4.4 - 0.5
#78124

Elementary Physics

Motion

BLACKBIRCH®
PRESS

THOMSON
™
GALE

San Diego • Detroit • New York • San Francisco • Cleveland • New Haven, Conn. • Waterville, Maine • London • Munich

THOMSON

✦ ™

GALE

For more information, contact
The Gale Group, Inc.
27500 Drake Rd.
Farmington Hills, MI 48331-3535
Or you can visit our Internet site at http://www.gale.com

Photo Credits: **Art I Need:** 4, 6, 12; **Corbis:** 1, 2t, 2b, 16, 18; **Daimler Chrysler:** 8; **Digital Vision:** 20; **Ford:** 14; **NASA:** 9.

Consultant: Don Franceschetti, Ph.D., Distinguished Service Professor, Departments of Physics and Chemistry, The University of Memphis, Memphis, Tennessee

For The Brown Reference Group plc
Text: Ben Morgan
Project Editor: Tim Harris
Picture Researcher: Helen Simm
Illustrations: Darren Awuah and Mark Walker
Designer: Alison Gardner
Design Manager: Jeni Child
Managing Editor: Bridget Giles
Production Director: Alastair Gourlay
Children's Publisher: Anne O'Daly
Editorial Director: Lindsey Lowe

LIBRARY OF CONGRESS CATALOGING-IN-PUBLICATION DATA

Morgan, Ben.
  Motion / by Ben Morgan.
    p. cm. — (Elementary physics)
Includes bibliographical references and index.
  ISBN 1-41030-082-X (hardback: alk. paper) — ISBN 1-41030-200-8 (paperback: alk. paper)
  1. Force and energy—Juvenile literature. 2. Machinery—Juvenile literature. [1. Motion.
2. Force and energy.] I. Title. II. Series: Morgan, Ben. Elementary physics.

  QC73.4.M65 2003
  531'.6—dc21   2003002020

Contents

As you hit a golf ball with a club,
a force makes the ball move.

What Is Force?

A push or pull is a **force**. If you give a toy car a push, the force from your hand starts it moving. When a baseball player strikes a ball, the force of the bat sends the ball hurtling away.

Small objects do not need much force to start moving fast. To make a marble roll, all you have to do is flick it gently. Large objects like cars and trains need a huge force to start moving quickly. That is why pushing a toy car is much easier than pushing a real car.

The force of gravity pulls skiers downhill.

Types of Forces

Forces that only work when objects touch are called **contact forces**. You use contact forces when you throw a ball, push a toy car, or ride a bicycle. Some forces work without touching anything. A **magnet**, for instance, can pull some metal objects toward itself without touching them. The magnet's invisible force is called **magnetism**.

Another invisible force is gravity. **Gravity** is the force that pulls things to the ground when you drop them. It also lets skiers shoot downhill without making any effort.

When a car accelerates, it goes faster.

Speeding Up

If you give an extra push to a moving object, it speeds up. The more **force** you apply to the object, the faster it goes. When something goes faster, it **accelerates**.

A cyclist can go faster and faster by pedaling hard, for instance. The force from the cyclist's feet makes the bicycle speed up. Another way to speed up is to cycle downhill. The force of **gravity** pulls on the bicycle and makes it go faster.

Air pushes against the parachute
of the space shuttle. This slows the
shuttle as it lands.

Slowing Down

Forces can slow things down as well as speed them up. If you push the front of a toy car while it is moving, the force makes it stop. If you catch a ball, the force from your hands stops the ball's movement. If the ball is traveling fast, you can really feel the force pushing your hands.

The space shuttle uses a parachute to slow it down when it lands. The parachute catches air, and the air pushes the parachute backward. This slows the forward movement of the shuttle.

Field-hockey players use their
sticks to hit the ball and change
the direction it is moving.

Changing Direction

Forces can also change the direction of moving objects. Tennis players force balls to change directions with their rackets. A skillful player can control exactly where the ball travels.

If you throw a ball in the air, it will go up, stop, then come down again. Force from your moving arm pushes it up. As it goes up, the force of Earth's **gravity** causes it to slow down and then come back downward.

A car crash in a test center shows
how inertia can throw the driver
forward during a sudden stop.

Inertia

Objects need **forces** to make them move differently. A moving object will keep moving unless a force stops it. If something is still, it will stay still unless a force moves it. This tendency to stay still or keep moving is called **inertia**. When you stop pedaling a bicycle, inertia keeps you going for a while.

Inertia can be dangerous. If you brake too suddenly while riding a bicycle, inertia can make you fall over the handlebars. When a car crashes or stops very suddenly, the people inside it can be thrown forward by inertia. That is why it is so important to wear a seatbelt.

Friction slows you as you come down a slide.

Friction

No matter how hard you push a toy car, it will always slow down and come to a stop after a while. The **force** that stops it is called **friction**. Friction happens whenever objects rub together. When you ride a bicycle, there is friction between the wheels and the ground. If you use the brakes, the brake pads rub the wheels and cause more friction.

When you go down a slide, there is friction between your body and the slide. On the steep part of the slide, **gravity** pulls you down quickly. On the level part of the slide, friction slows you down.

Overcoming Friction

Friction often slows things down. People have come up with ways to overcome friction, though. Wheels are one way to overcome friction. Shopping carts and wheelbarrows both use wheels to make carrying a heavy weight much easier. Just think how hard it would be to drag a load of bricks along the ground.

Machines with moving parts often have oil to reduce friction. A rusty old bicycle will travel much faster if you put oil on its **chain** and **cogs**.

Left: A skater moves fast because the skate blades melt the top layer of ice. Since water causes less friction than ice, the skates are not slowed very much.

A hammer increases the
force of a person's hand.

Tools and Machines

Tools are things that increase **forces**. They make some tasks much easier. **Wrenches**, for instance, make it easier to loosen stiff **bolts**. Unscrewing a bolt with your bare hands is very hard work. If you use a wrench, you increase the force of your hands, and the job becomes easier to do.

Machines also increase force. They are more complicated than tools. Machines contain moving parts that change and increase forces. A bicycle is a machine. It changes the up-and-down movements of your feet on the pedals into a forward push that moves the bicycle.

Spinning Egg Trick

Here is a trick to show the effects of **inertia**. You need a hardboiled egg and a raw egg. Shuffle them around until you cannot tell which is which. Then spin each egg on a plate. When you have got the hang of spinning them, quickly and gently stop the eggs and let go. The raw egg will start spinning again but the boiled egg will not.

The experiment works because the insides of the raw egg have their own inertia. When you stop the raw egg from spinning, its liquid insides keep moving. After you let go, the inertia of the insides makes the raw egg start spinning again.

Glossary

acceleration a change in the speed of an object.

bolt a metal rod for joining objects.

chain a series of metal links that turns the wheels of a bicycle.

cog a tooth on the rim of a metal wheel that turns a chain.

contact force a force that works when two or more objects touch.

force any action that changes the shape or movement of an object.

friction the force that slows down moving objects that are touching.

gravity the pulling force that attracts objects to each other.

inertia the tendency of objects to resist a change in their movement.

machine an object that helps make work easier.

magnet an object that can attract certain metals.

magnetism the force created by a magnet.

wrench a tool for holding, twisting, or turning an object.

Look Further

To find out more experiments you can carry out with force and motion, read *101 Great Science Experiments* by Neil Ardley (DK Publishing). You can also find out more about force and motion from the internet at these websites:

www.kapili.com/physics4kids/motion/force.html

www.energyquest.ca.gov/story/index.html

Index

OCT 28 '98

FOLLETT